PSYCHOLOGY OF LIFE

Truth and Tips

Anirudha Singh

NOTION PRESS

Contact:
Anirudha Singh (Author)
Email: authoranirudha@gmail.com
Instagram: @anirudhasingh24
X (Twitter): @anirudhasingh24

ISBN-10: 1639572104 (Paperback)
ISBN-13: 978-1639572106 (Paperback)
ISBN-13: 979-8894755830 (Hardcover)

Latest printing edition 2024.

Contents

Psychology of Life

TRUTH

"You change for two reasons: Either you learn enough that you want to, or you've been hurt enough that you have to."

1. If we have a plan B, our plan A is less likely to work.

Every now and then, it hurts to be prepared. In a series of experiments from the University of Pennsylvania, researchers found that when volunteers thought about a backup plan before starting a task, they did worse than those who hadn't thought about a plan B. What's more, when they realized they had options, their motivation for succeeding the first time around dropped. The researchers stress that thinking ahead is a good idea, but you might be more successful if you keep those plans vague.

2. Fear can feel good—if we're not really in danger.

Not everyone loves scary movies, but for the people who do, there are a few theories as to why—the main one coming down to hormones. When you're watching a scary movie or walking through a haunted house, you get all the adrenaline, endorphins, and dopamine from a fight-or-flight response, but no matter how scared you feel, your brain recognizes that you're not really in danger—so you get that natural high without the risk.

3. "Catching" a yawn could help us bond.

Why do you yawn when someone else does, even if you aren't tired? There are a few theories about why yawning is contagious, but one of the leading ones is that it shows empathy.

People who are less likely to show empathy—such as toddlers who haven't learned it yet or young people with autism— are also less likely to yawn in reaction to someone else's.

4. We care more about a single person than about massive tragedies.

In another University of Pennsylvania study, one group learned about a little girl who was starving to death, another learned about millions dying of hunger, and a third learned about both situations. People donated more than twice as much money when hearing about the little girl than when hearing the statistics—and even the group who'd heard her story in the context of the bigger tragedy donated less. Psychologists think that we're wired to help the person in front of us, but when the problem feels too big, we figure our little part isn't doing much.

5. Beginnings and ends are easier to remember than middles.

When people are asked to recall items from a list, they're most likely to think of things from the very end, or from the very beginning, found one study published in *Frontiers of Human Neuroscience*. The middle gets muddled, which could also play into why you remember your boss wrapping up her presentation, but not so much about the middle.

6. It takes five positive things to outweigh a single negative thing.

Our brains have something called a "negativity bias" that makes us remember bad news more than good, which is why you quickly forget that your co- workers complimented your presentation but keep dwelling on the fact that a kid at the bus stop insulted your shoes. To feel balanced, we need at least a five to one ration of good to bad in our lives.

7. Food tastes better when someone else makes it.

Ever wonder why that sandwich from the takeout place down the street tastes better than the ones you make at home, even if you use the same ingredients? One study published in the journal *Science* found that when you make yourself a meal, you're around it so long that it feels less exciting by the time you actually dig in—and that, subsequently, decreases your enjoyment.

8. We'd rather know something bad is coming than not know what to expect.

Researchers who published their work in the journal *Nature* have found that it's less stressful to know something negative is about to happen (e.g., there's no chance we'll get to a meeting on time) than when we don't know how things will work out (e.g., we might be on time after all). That's because the part of our brain that predicts consequences—

whether good or bad—is most active when it doesn't know what to expect. If stepping on the gas will help us beat traffic, we'll go through that stress instead of just accepting that we'll have to come up with a decent excuse when (not if) we're late.

9. We always try to return a favour.

It's not just good manners—the "rule of reciprocity" suggests that we're programmed to want to help someone who's helped us. It probably developed because, to keep society working smoothly, people need to help each other out. Stores (and some frenemies) like to use this against you, offering freebies in hopes that you'll spend some cash.

10. When one rule seems too strict, we want to break more.

Psychologists have studied a phenomenon called reactance: When people perceive certain freedoms being taken away, they not only break that rule, but they break even more than they otherwise would have in an effort to regain their freedom. This could be one of the best psychology facts to explain why a teenager who can't use his phone in class will chew gum while stealthily sending a text.

11. Our favorite subject is ourselves.

Don't blame your self-absorbed brother for talking about himself—it's just the way his brain is wired. The reward centres of our brains light up more when we're talking about ourselves than when we're talking about other people, according to a Harvard study.

12. There's a reason we want to squeeze cute things.

"It's so cute, I just was to smooch it until it pops!" That's called cuteness aggression, and people who feel it don't really want to crush that adorable puppy. Research published in *Frontiers in Behavioural Neuroscience* found that when we're feeling overwhelmed by positive emotions—like we do when looking at an impossibly cute baby animal—a little bit of aggression helps us balance out that high.

13. Our brains try to make boring speeches more interesting.

University of Glasgow researchers found that in the same way that we hear voices in our heads when we read aloud, our brains also "talk" over boring speeches. If someone is speaking monotonously, we'll subconsciously make it more vivid in our heads.

14. Some people enjoy seeing anger in others.

In one University of Michigan study, people with high testosterone remembered information better when it was paired with an angry face than a neutral one or no face, indicating they found the angry glare rewarding. The researchers said it could mean that certain people enjoy making someone else glare at them—as long the flash of anger doesn't last long enough to be a threat—which could be why that guy in the office won't let go of that stupid joke at your expense.

15. We automatically second-guess ourselves when other people disagree.

In a famous 1950s experiment, college students were asked to point out which of three lines was the same length as a fourth. When they heard others (who were in on the experiment) choose an answer that was clearly wrong, the participants followed their lead and gave that same wrong answer.

16. We aren't as good at multitasking as we think we are.

Research published in the *Journal of Experimental Psychology* shows that even when you think you're doing two things at once, what you're actually doing is switching quickly between the two tasks—you're still focusing on one at a time. No wonder it's so hard to listen to your partner while scrolling through Instagram.

17. We're convinced that the future is bright.

Doesn't matter if you like where you're at right now or not—most of us have an "optimism bias" that convinces us the future will be better than the present, according to research in *Current Biology*.

We assume we'll rise up in our careers, never get divorced, raise little angels of children, and live to a ripe old age. Those might not all be realistic for everyone, but there's no harm in dreaming.

18. We (unintentionally) believe what we want to believe.

Humans are victim to something called confirmation bias: the tendency to interpret facts in a way that confirms what we already believe. So, no matter how many facts you throw at your uncle trying to sway his political opinions, there's a good chance he isn't going to budge. It's one of the psychology facts you'll just have to accept that you can't change.

19. Our brains want us to be lazy.

Evolutionarily speaking, conserving energy is a good thing—when food was scarce, our ancestors still had to be ready for anything. Unfortunately for anyone watching their weight, that still holds true today. A small study published in *Current Biology* found that when walking on a treadmill, volunteers would automatically adjust their gait to burn fewer calories.

20. Being lonely is bad for our health.

Researchers found that the fewer friends a person has, the higher levels of the blood-clotting protein fibrinogen. The effect was so strong that having 15 friends instead of 25 was just as bad as smoking.

21. You're programmed to love the music you listened to in high school the most.

The music we like gives us a hit of dopamine and other feel-good chemicals, and that's even stronger when we're young because our brains are developing. From around age 12 to 22, everything feels more important, so we tend to emphasize those years the most and hang on to those musical memories.

"Researchers have uncovered evidence that suggests our brains bind us to the music we heard as teenagers more tightly than anything we'll hear as adults—a connection that doesn't weaken as we age," writes Mark Joseph Stern for *Slate*.

22. Memories are more like pieced-together pictures than accurate snapshots.

Even people with the best memories in the world can have "false memories." The brain generally remembers the gist of what happens, then fills in the rest—sometimes inaccurately—which explains why you insist your wife was with you at a party six years ago, even though she's adamant she wasn't.

23. There's a reason that certain color combinations are hard on your eyes.

When you see bright blue and red right next to each other, your brain thinks the red is closer than the blue, making you go practically cross-eyed. Same goes for other combinations, like red and green.

24. Putting information in bite-sized pieces helps us remember.

Your short-term memory can only hold on to so much information at a time (unless you try one of the simple ways to improve your memory), which is why you use "chunking" to remember long numbers. For instance, if you try to memorize this number: 90655372, you probably naturally thought something like 906-553-72.

25. You remember things better if you've been tested on them.

Sorry, kids! One of the most useful psychology facts is that testing really does work. One study published in the journal *Psychological Science* found that people are more likely to store information in their long-term memory if they've been tested on the information (the more, the better) than if they just study and don't need to remember it right away.

26. Too much choice can become paralyzing.

The whole "paradox of choice" theory has been criticized by researchers who say it hasn't been shown in studies, but there is some evidence that our brains prefer a few options to a ton. When singles at speed-dating events met more people and those people had more diversity in factors like age and occupation, the participants chose fewer potential dates.

27. When you feel like you're low on something (like money), you obsess over it.

Psychologists have found that the brain is sensitive to scarcity—the feeling that you're missing something you need. When farmers have a good cash flow, for instance, they tend to be better planners than when they're tight for money, one study found. When you're feeling cash-strapped, you might need more reminders to pay bills or do chores because your mind is too busy to remember.

28. We keep believing things, even when we know they're wrong.

Researchers in one *Science* study fed volunteers false information, then a week later revealed that the facts weren't actually true. Even though the volunteers knew the truth (now), fMRI scans showed that they still believed the misinformation about half the time. It's one of the psychology facts to know that could make you smarter.

29. We look for human faces, even in inanimate objects.

Most of us haven't seen Jesus in a piece of toast, but we've all noticed cartoonish faces seemingly staring back at us from inanimate objects. That's called pareidolia, and scientists think it comes from the fact that recognizing faces is so important to social life that our brains would rather find one where there isn't one than miss a real-life face.

30. We will always, always, always find a problem.

Ever wonder why when one problem resolves, another one takes its place? It's not that the world is against you—but your brain might be, in a sense. Researchers asked volunteers to pick out threatening-looking people from computer-generated faces. "As we showed people fewer and fewer threatening faces over time, we found that they expanded their definition of 'threatening' to include a wider range of faces," writes researcher David Levari, PhD. "In other words, when they ran out of threatening faces to find, they started calling faces threatening that they used to call harmless."

31. We'd rather skew the facts than change our beliefs about people.

Humans hate "cognitive dissonance": when a fact counters something we believe. That's why when, we hear that a loved one did something wrong or garbage, we undermine how bad it really was, or we tell ourselves that science exaggerates when a study tells us we really need to move more.

32. People rise to our high expectations (and don't rise if we have low ones).

You may have heard of the Pygmalion effect before— basically, we do well when other people think we will, and we don't do well when people expect us to fail. The idea came from a famous 1960s study in which researchers told teachers that certain students (chosen at random) had high potential based on IQ tests. Those students did indeed go on to be high achievers, thanks to their teachers' expectations in them.

33. Social media is psychologically designed to be addictive.

Told yourself you'd just quickly check your Facebook notifications, and 15 minutes later you're still scrolling? You're not alone. Part of that has to do with infinite scroll: When you can stay on the site without actually interacting and clicking, your brain doesn't get that "stop" cue.

34. We can convince ourselves a boring task was fun if we weren't rewarded.

Here's another great example of cognitive dissonance: Volunteers in one *Psychology of Learning and Motivation* study did a boring task, then were paid either $1 or $20 to convince someone that it was actually pretty interesting. The ones who were paid $20 knew why they'd lied (they got a decent reward) and still thought it was boring, but the ones who'd only gotten a buck actually convinced themselves it really was fun, because their brains didn't have a good reason to think they'd been lying.

35. Power makes people care less about others.

You've probably heard about the famous Stanford prison experiment. (Refresher: College students were randomly assigned to be either a prisoner or guard in a fake prison, and the "guards" started harassing the "prisoners." It got so bad that the two-week experiment was cancelled after six days.). That's pretty extreme, but later studies have found that when people feel like they're in a power position, they become worse at judging a person's feelings based on their facial expressions, indicating a loss of empathy.

36. To our ancestors, sugar and fat were good things.

Why, oh why, does cake have to taste better than vegetables? Well, because that's how we were primed for millions of years. For our ancestors, getting a quick hit of energy from sugar and then storing it as fat, or eating plenty of fat to keep our bodies and brains fuelled meant more energy in the long run. But now that sugary, fatty foods are easy (a little too easy) to eat and overeat, our bodies are still primed to store that fat—even though we don't need it.

37. Our brain doesn't think long-term deadlines are so important.

Pretty much everyone has procrastinated at one time or another, even though we know logically that it would make more sense to get a jump on our taxes than to turn on Netflix. We prefer urgent, unimportant tasks because we know we'll be able to complete them. There's also evidence that when we see the deadline looming in terms of days, rather than months or years, because we feel more connected to a day-by-day passing of time.

38. We loosen our morals when an authority tells us to.

It's one of the oldest psychology facts in the books: In the 1960s, Yale psychologist Stanley Milgram infamously conducted an experiment that he thought would prove Americans wouldn't accept immoral orders like the Nazis had. For a "learning task," volunteers were told to deliver shocks to a "learner" (an actor, little known to the real volunteers) if they got an answer wrong. To Milgram's horror, the participants continued delivering shocks, even when the learner screamed in pain.

39. Money can buy happiness, but only up to a certain point.

Research shows that in terms of income, people have a "satiation point" where happiness peaks and earning more won't actually make you happier. Different studies have suggested various amounts (one 2010 study said $75,000, but a 2018 survey said $105,000), but the point is the same: Constantly aiming for more, more, more won't necessarily do you any good.

40. It's not just how much money we make, it's how we spend it.

Even if you haven't topped out to your happiest income, your money can still determine your happiness. You've probably already heard about research that shows we're more satisfied when we spend money on experiences (a nice meal out or theatre tickets) than on possessions because it helps us socialize and feel more alive. But another study published in *Science* found another strategy for using money the most satisfying way: spending on other people instead of ourselves.

Tips

"It all depends on how we look at things"

1. Look into someone's eyes when you get a dissatisfactory answer.

Sometimes we don't like the answer to a question that we receive and sometimes we don't understand it. Instead of repeating the question or asking another, look into the eyes of the person. This will make the person feel under pressure or cornered, and this will force them to further elaborate their thoughts.

2. Stay calm when someone raises their voice to you.

Make a strong effort to remain calm. When a loudmouth acts out it's usually in anger, and our behaviours can sometimes unintentionally provoke that. The feelings of anger usually quickly subside and guilt will set in and usually this person is first to ask for forgiveness.

3. Sit close to the aggressor to avoid attack.

If you're heading into a meeting and you know you'll be in the room with an aggressive person, you know the discussion may become heated, or you may be subjected to negative criticism, make a point to sit next to that person. You may feel uncomfortable and awkward, but you won't be the only one. Close proximity is known to make people uncomfortable which will lessen the level of aggression they plan to exercise.

4. Remember everyone's names if you want to be popular.

If you want to be popular with your peers and colleagues, make it a habit to start calling people by their first names when speaking with them. A person feels instantaneously special when you call him or her by their first name.

5. Write down your thoughts when you feel stressed or anxious.

We all feel some level of mental stress or anxiety at some point. Write down your thoughts in a journal and then close it up. Believe it or not, you'll be able to focus on your work more easily because you have now shared your thoughts with someone. When you share them, you will then feel the burden on your mind reduced.

6. Give yourself fewer choices when you can't make the decision.

Some people believe that it's better to have more choices and more information and actually, they prefer to have more. However, it is actually paralyzing to have too many. There is evidence that shows that having four options at a time is the maximum number we can consider and still make a choice. In order to be an effective decision maker, you should only give yourself a few options at a time. This will allow you time to consider each one while giving you enough space between looking at a new set of options.

7. Right posture can boost confidence.

This psychological trick applies to both work and pleasure. It can drastically improve your dating life and help you move up the ladder at work. How can you become confident do you ask? The best way to do this is through your posture. If you allow yourself to take up more space, you're more likely to feel more confident. This is referred to power language.

8. Sure-fire way to win in 'rock, paper, scissors'.

This one is definitely intriguing. When you're about to play this famous game, ask your opponent a random question right before. This typically will throw your confused opponent off and more often than not they will throw up 'scissors'.

9. Make people feel needed when you ask for help.

If you need someone's help start off with the phrase, 'I need your help...' People like to feel needed and they hate feeling guilty. By starting off the conversation with that phrase, you're more likely to receive the help you need.

10. Warm your hands before shaking hands with others.

Did you know that cold hands are linked to distrust? When you're about to touch someone or shake their hand, make sure that your hands are warm. Warm hands promote a friendly atmosphere.

Other psychological tricks

- If you think someone doesn't care for you, ask him or her to borrow their pen or pencil.

- If you can't seem to get a song out of your head try remembering the end of it.

- If you need help carrying something, try talking to the person while handing them whatever it is. They will most likely not even realize you're handing them something and they will just take it.

- During an introduction, make a note of someone's eye color. You're not going to use this information it's just important to take note of it. It's a technique to achieve optimum eye contact. People find this friendly and confident.

Improve Listening Skills

We have two ears and one mouth for a reason—effective communication is dependent on using them in proportion, and this involves having good listening skills.

The workplace of the 21st century may not look the same as it did before COVID-19 spread throughout the world like wildfire, but that doesn't mean you can relax your standards at work. If anything, Zoom meetings, conference calls, and the continuous time spent behind a screen have created a higher level of expectations for meeting etiquette and communication. And this goes further than simply muting your microphone during a meeting.

Effective workplace communication has been a topic of discussion for decades, yet, it is rarely addressed or implemented due to a lack of awareness and personal ownership by all parties.

Effective communication isn't just about speaking clearly or finding the appropriate choice of words. It starts with intentional listening and being present. Here's how to improve your listening skills for effective workplace communication.

Listen to Understand, Not to Speak

There are stark differences between listening and hearing. Listening involves intention, focused effort, and concentration, whereas hearing simply involves low-level awareness that someone else is speaking. Listening is a voluntary activity that allows one to be present and in the moment while hearing is passive and effortless.

Which one would you prefer your colleagues to implement during your company-wide presentation? It's a no-brainer.

Listening can be one of the most powerful tools in your communication arsenal because one must listen to understand the message being told to them. As a result of this deeper understanding, communication can be streamlined because there is a higher level of comprehension that will facilitate practical follow-up questions, conversations, and problem-solving. And just because you heard something doesn't mean you actually understood it.

We take this for granted daily, but that doesn't mean we can use that as an excuse.

Your brain is constantly scanning your environment for threats, opportunities, and situations to advance your ability to promote your survival. And yet, while we are long past the days of worrying about being eaten by wildlife, the neurocircuitry responsible for these mechanisms is still hard-wired into our psychology and neural processing.

A classic example of this is the formation of memories. Case in point: where were you on June 3rd, 2014? For most of you reading this article, your mind will go completely blank, which isn't necessarily bad.

The brain is far too efficient to retain every detail about every event that happens in your life, mainly because many events that occur aren't always that important. The brain doesn't—and shouldn't—care what you ate for lunch three weeks ago or what color shirt you wore golfing last month. But for those of you who remember where you were on June 3rd,

2014, this date probably holds some sort of significance to you.

Maybe it was a birthday or an anniversary. Perhaps it was the day your child was born. It could have even been a day where you lost someone special in your life.

Regardless of the circumstance, the brain is highly stimulated through emotion and engagement, which is why memories are usually stored in these situations. When the brain's emotional centres become activated, the brain is far more likely to remember an event. And this is also true when intention and focus are applied to listening to a conversation. Utilizing these hard-wired primitive pathways of survival to optimize your communication in the workplace is a no-brainer—literally and figuratively.

Intentional focus and concentrated efforts will pay off in the long run because you will retain more information and have an easier time recalling it down the road, making you look like a superstar in front of your colleagues and co- workers.

Effective Communication Isn't Always Through Words

While we typically associate communication with words and verbal affirmations, communication can come in all shapes and forms. In the Zoom meeting era we live in, it has become far more challenging to utilize and understand these other forms of language. And this is because they are typically easier to see when we are sitting face to face with the person we speak to.

Body language can play a significant role in how our words and communication are interpreted, especially when there is a disconnection involved. When someone tells you one thing, yet their body language screams something completely different, it's challenging to let that go. Our brain immediately starts to search for more information and inevitably prompts us to follow up with questions that will provide greater clarity to the situation at hand. And in all reality, not saying something might be just as important as actually saying something.

These commonly overlooked non-verbal communication choices can provide a plethora of information about the intentions, emotions, and motivations. We do this unconsciously, and it happens with every confrontation, conversation, and interaction we engage in. The magic lies in the utilization and active interpretation of these signals to improve your listening skills and your communication skills.

Our brains were designed for interpreting our world, which is why we are so good at recognizing subtle nuances and underlying disconnect within our casual encounters. So, when we begin to notice conflicting messages between verbal and non-verbal communication, our brain takes us down a path of troubleshooting.

Which messages are consistent with this theme over time? Which statements aren't aligning with what they're really trying to tell me? How should I interpret their words and body language?

Suppose we want to break things down even further. In that case, one must understand that body language is usually a subconscious event, meaning that we rarely think about our body language. This happens because our brain's primary focus is to string together words and phrases for verbal communication, which usually requires a higher level of processing. This doesn't mean that body language will always tell the truth, but it does provide clues to help us weigh information, which can be pretty beneficial in the long run.

Actively interpreting body language can provide you with an edge in your communication skills. It can also be used as a tool to connect with the individual you are speaking to. This process is deeply ingrained into our human fabric and utilizes similar methods babies use while learning new skills from their parents' traits during the early years of development.

Mirroring a person's posture or stance can create a subtle bond, facilitating a sense of feeling like one another. This process is triggered via the activation of specific brain regions through the stimulation of specialized neurons called mirror neurons. These particular neurons become activated while watching an individual engage in an activity or task, facilitating learning, queuing, and understanding. They also allow the person watching an action to become more efficient at physically executing the action, creating changes in the brain, and altering the overall structure of the brain to enhance output for that chosen activity.

Listening with intention can make you understand your colleague, and when paired together with mirroring body language, you can make your colleague feel like you two are alike. This simple trick can facilitate a greater bond of understanding and communication within all aspects of the conversation.

Eliminate All Distractions, Once and for All

As Jim Rohn says, "What is easy to do is also easy not to do." And this is an underlying principle that will carry through in all aspects of communication. Distractions are a sure-fire way to ensure a lack of understanding or interpretation of a conversation, which in turn, will create inefficiencies and a poor foundation for communication.

This should come as no surprise, especially in this day in age where people are constantly distracted by social media, text messaging, and endlessly checking their emails. We're stuck in a cultural norm that has hijacked our love for the addictive dopamine rush and altered our ability to truly focus our efforts on the task at hand. And these distractions aren't just distractions for the time they're being used.

They use up coveted brainpower and central processes that secondarily delay our ability to get back on track.

Gloria Mark, a researcher at UC Irvine, discovered that it takes an average of 23 minutes and 15 seconds for our brains to reach their peak state of focus after an interruption. Yes, you read that correctly—distractions are costly, error-prone, and yield little to no benefit outside of a bump to the ego when receiving a new like on your social media profile.

Meetings should implement a no-phone policy, video conference calls should be set on their own browser with no other tabs open, and all updates, notifications, and email prompt should be immediately turned off, if possible, to eliminate all distractions during a meeting.

These are just a few examples of how we can optimize our environment to facilitate the highest levels of communication within the workplace.

Actions Speak Louder Than Words

Effective communication in the workplace doesn't have to be challenging, but it does have to be intentional. Knowledge can only take us so far, but once again, knowing something is very different than putting it into action.

Just like riding a bike, the more often you do it, the easier it becomes. Master communicators are phenomenal listeners, which allows them to be effective communicators in the workplace and in life. If you genuinely want to own your communication, you must implement this information today and learn how to improve your listening skills.

Choose your words carefully, listen intently, and most of all, be present in the moment—because that's what master communicators do, and you can do it, too!

END